D0564631

Database 101

Database 101

Guy Kawasaki

An Open House Book

Peachpit Press, Inc.

Database 101
Guy Kawasaki

Peachpit Press, Inc., 2414 Sixth St., Berkeley, CA 94710
(415) 548-4393; (415) 548-5991 (fax)

Notice of Liability:

Trademarks:

ISBN 0-938151-52-5
0 9 8 7 6 5 4 3 2 1

Printed and bound in the United States of America

*To Jud Spencer and Danny Cooley, the
authors of TouchBASE, and the other
third-generation Macintosh programmers
who keep Selling the Dream.*

Contents

Just the Way It Is

When I first self-published *The Little Mac Book* and *The Mac is not a typewriter*, I was told by several of my peers that the books were too informal, that they would not be accepted by the business world. I published them as they were anyway because I firmly believed in what I learned from teaching Macintosh courses: people are people, no matter what sort of business they are in, and everyone enjoys the learning process more if it is fun. That's just the way it is.

In my Intro to Mac classes, I find it so thrilling to see people's attitudes change. They often come in a little intimidated about computers. I love to watch the Macintosh Phenomenon take place: within weeks, these intimidated people are trying to think up work to do just so they can use the Mac. Who ever heard of such a thing? What other tool inspires people to *create* work for themselves?

Using a database was the most eye-opening concept to the most people. Originally, databases were also the most terrifying. They terrified *me* at first; the terms sounded so high-tech (some of you are laughing—hey, they *do* sound high-tech if you've never been exposed to them!). But the Macintosh Phenomenon kicked in: the darn things were actually fun. And my classes had fun with them. Literally *everyone* could make their life easier with a database. What would I do without my database of the people I invite to my parties?

A problem with databases for most people lies in that intimidation factor: what the heck *is* a database anyway? Guy solves that problem. In this delightful little book, Guy is able to make the concept, the usefulness, even the practical steps, approachable to absolutely anyone. And he does it with fun, with wit, with style. As many of us are aware, Guy has a personable, charming way about him.

Reading this book is like having him chatting with you over coffee, patiently explaining the entire process from start to finish, in clear, concise steps, always with a smile on his face, always putting a smile on your face. You can't help but enjoy it. You can't help but see that your life also needs a database. You can't help but feel that you could *easily* create a useful, functional database and have fun doing it. Put Guy and the Macintosh together and that's what happens. That's just the way it is.

—*Robin Williams*

> If you would not be forgotten as soon as you are
> dead, either write things worth reading or do things
> worth writing.
>
> —Benjamin Franklin

The Book for
the Rest of Us

Key concepts

- Intended market

- Guy's background

- Contact management

XV
DB101

Who Should Read This Book

You should buy this book if you don't know much about databases and want to learn more. Maybe you are too embarrassed to ask others. Maybe you can't find anyone who knows enough about databases to help you. Maybe you just want to understand databases before you buy one.

I've slanted this book toward Macintosh databases. Nevertheless, my good friend Bill Gates, chairman of Microsoft, tells me that all computers will soon look alike, so it should also be helpful to owners of those other computers running Windows.

My Background

Back in 1983 I was a software evangelist at Apple Computer, and my job was to make sure that Macintosh had a lot of software. Maybe I went overboard in the database category because there were soon about 10 Macintosh databases including PFS: File, OverVUE, Filevision, Microsoft File, Helix, DB Master, MacLion, Hayden Base, and Interlace.

In 1987 I believed my own hype about the opportunities in the Macintosh software market and left Apple to start a company called ACIUS. It had a database product called 4th Dimension. I quickly learned what it's like to be a Macintosh software developer: it's not that easy.

Now it's 1991. I left ACIUS (it's a long story), and I'm semi-retired. I read a book called *The Mac is not a typewriter* by Robin Williams that explains the basics of Macintosh typography to "the rest of us." It inspired me to write this book to try to explain databases to the rest of us.

Managing Contacts

One of the most common uses of a database is to keep track of personal and business contacts. Since this is a straightforward example for most people, I've chosen it as a framework for this book.

I use a product called TouchBASE to keep track of my contacts. It is the Sony Walkman of Macintosh databases: small, dedicated to single purpose, and relatively inexpensive ($125 suggested retail).

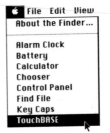

I like TouchBASE so much that I invested in the product. If imitation is the sincerest form of flattery, investment is the sincerest form of product endorsement.

Throughout the book I use TouchBASE and FileMaker Pro to provide screen shots and examples. FileMaker Pro is an entry-level database from Claris Corporation. It is probably the best-selling Macintosh database.

Though I use TouchBASE and FileMaker Pro in this book, the principles and concepts that I explain are common to most personal computer databases.

Acknowledgments

My thanks to the beta test gang: Basil Bourque, Bill Bowmer, Walt Campbell, Barry Cohen, Joe Friend, Larry Glazerman, Don Haupt, Robert Kline, Edward Kramer, Brien Lee, Len Macdonell, Dennis Marshall, George McCluney, Mark Metzger, Paul Miller, Rick Monteverde, Joe Nartowicz, Daniel Sefton, Ava Weintraub, and Richard Williams.

Special thanks to Will Mayall and Terry Lonier. They had the most influence on the form and content of this book.

Finally, thanks to Nancy Tobin, Steve Roth, Susie Hammond, and Ole Kvern. Nancy created the wacky illustrations for this book. Steve, Susie, and Ole took my unpolished text, refined it, and turned it into a book.

> To his dog, every man is Napoleon; hence the constant popularity of dogs.
>
> Aldous Huxley

What Is a Database?

Key concepts

- Database
- Database files
- Records
- Fields

Introduction

This chapter defines what a database is and other essential database elements. After reading it, you should have a basic knowledge of database terminology.

What Is a Database?

Imagine that you gathered all the business cards, ledger cards, and scraps of paper that contain information about your personal and business contacts. Having collected this mishmash of stuff, you decide to organize all the information into a more useful form.

You could make a list of the people on sheets of paper, but then you couldn't shuffle the information around. What if you wanted to group together all the people who worked at the same company? What if you wanted to look at your contacts alphabetically by last name?

A better idea is to make one information sheet for each person, where each information sheet has the same format so that first names, last names, and company names are always in the same place.

Then you could take all the information sheets and place them in a binder. Even a binder is an improvement over a list because you can take information sheets out of the binder and put them back in different places.

What is a database? It's a file that's an electronic version of information sheets and binders. It enables you to efficiently use your information. With a database, you can manage projects large or small, professional or personal. Below are examples of the things a database will enable you to do.

❏ Maintain the roster of your PTA, church, or environmental group.

❏ Track sales leads for your real estate, Amway, or Tupperware business.

❏ Categorize your collection of CDs, records, tapes, or books.

❏ Monitor contributors and supporters of a political candidate or campaign.

❏ Bill and track payments of shipments for a small business.

Database Terminology 101

Just as a binder contains information sheets, a database file holds records.

In computerese, information sheets are called records. Each record contains data about one person, so, for example, 1,000 records in a database file are the equivalent of 1,000 information sheets.

Records, in turn, are made up of fields. A field is an area that stores a discrete chunk of information such as someone's first name, last name, or company.

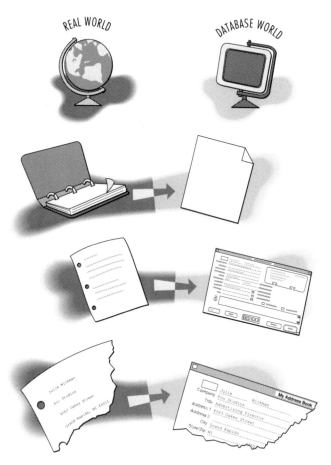

Table 1–1 compares the concepts of the database world to their real world counterparts.

Table 1–1 Real world and database world analogies

Real World	Database World
Binder	Database file
Information sheet	Record
Chunk of information	Field

Databases as Pets

You may find this weird, but there is one more way to define a database. It's an electronic pet—like a loyal and affectionate cat or dog. Unlike most other computer programs, a database is a living organism. It grows and requires nurture and care.

Word-processing and desktop-publishing programs produce things. You use these programs to make documents as-good-as-you-can or as-good-as-you-have-to (or time runs out), and then you print them. After that you store them away like old clothes.

By contrast, using a database is a process, not an event. When you are "one" with your database, you'll enter information into it every day. It will make you more productive and creative. You'll come to think of it more as a pet than as a thing—Zen and the Art of Database Management.

Test Drive a Database

The best way to understand a database is to use one, so there is a disk in the back of this book that contains demo versions of TouchBASE and FileMaker Pro. I've provided them so that you can get hands-on experience to understand better how databases work.

Summary

Was that so tough? Congratulations. You probably now know more about databases than most computer store clerks.

Quiz

1. Connect the database counterpart to the real world item.

Real World	**Database World**
Binder	Field
Information sheet	Record
Chunk of information	Database file

2. How is a database like a pet?

    ❑ Both need nurture and care

    ❑ Both need to be slapped around once in a while

    ❑ Both can make a mess on your carpet

3. A database is better than a binder because

    ❑ Binders rust

    ❑ Databases cost more

    ❑ Databases are more flexible and powerful

    ❑ Databases are topics for books

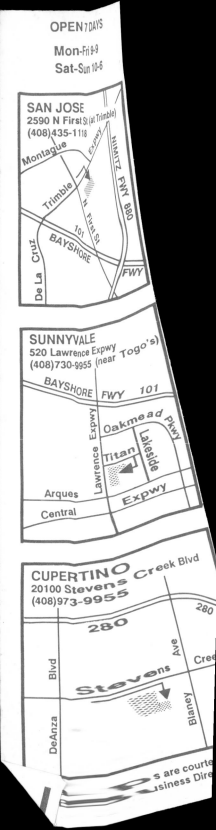

OPEN 7 DAYS

Mon-Fri 9-9
Sat-Sun 10-6

SAN JOSE
2590 N First St (at Trimble)
(408)435-1118

Montague
Trimble
N First St
Montague Expwy
NIMITZ FWY 880
101
BAYSHORE
De La Cruz
FWY

SUNNYVALE
520 Lawrence Expwy (near Togo's)
(408)730-9955

BAYSHORE FWY 101
Lawrence Expwy
Oakmead Pkwy
Lakeside
Titan
Arques
Central
Expwy

CUPERTINO
20100 Stevens Creek Blvd
(408)973-9955

280
280
Blvd
Stevens Ave
Cree
Stevens
Blaney
DeAnza

s are courte
usiness Dire

DB101 Quiz

1. Choose some reasons to use a database.

   ❏ You want to help database company executives buy fancy cars

   ❏ You want to save time

   ❏ You want to do things better

   ❏ You want to impress your friends

2. Choose the ways that you could use a database.

   ❏ As a tax deduction

   ❏ As a way to use up your quarterly budget for "toys"

   ❏ As a way to work better, faster, and easier

3. How many pieces of junk (a.k.a. "nonpersonalized") mail do you bother to read?

> *Nobody can count themselves an artist unless they can carry a picture in their head before they paint it.*
> *—Claude Monet*

Designing a Database

Key concepts

- Database content and structure

- Layouts

- Field types

Introduction

This chapter explains the process of designing a database. After reading it, you should understand how to create a database structure.

The Design Process

Databases usually require you to provide two things: content and structure—in other words, the information and the framework that the information goes into. A word processor, by contrast, provides the structure (the blank page) and requires only the content (the text that you type in).

Designing a database is an art: you pick from a palette of files, fields, and graphic tools to create a structure. Conceptually, the process is similar to setting up a binder. (The similarity quickly ends, however, because a database is much more flexible and powerful than a binder.) Designing a database is a three-step process.

Picturing the Database in Your Mind

The first step of designing a database is deciding on what information you want to store in the database. Do you want names? Addresses? Companies? Salaries? Pictures? Prices? As Monet would say, you have to picture the database in your mind to design it.

Creating Fields

The second step is to create fields in your file. This requires determining what types of fields you want. For example, fields can store text, numbers, pictures, or other kinds of data. (We'll discuss field types in the next section.)

might, for example, record the time and date that you called a sales prospect.

These fields are neither text nor numeric. They're not text fields because you may need to calculate the days between two dates or hours between two times. They're not number fields because making these calculations is not simple arithmetic—you cannot subtract January 1, 1991 from February 1, 1991.

Picture Fields

Picture fields are a Macintosh invention—or at least Macintosh made picture fields a mainstream field type. (It's difficult to imagine a picture in an MS-DOS database. You'd have to make it with Xs and Os.) Picture fields hold items such as scanned images and art created with drawing programs. A personnel database, for example, may contain pictures of employees.

Calculation and Summary Fields

Calculation and summary fields are fields that your database fills in for you. That is, you do not enter data into them. A calculation field is the result of operations such as adding, subtracting, multiplying, or dividing other fields. For example, a Cost field may be the product of price times quantity.

A summary field is the result of operations such as totaling, averaging, counting, or computing the minimum, maximum, or average of a number field in your database. A summary field, for example, of a Salary field may provide the average of all salaries in the database.

The Care and Feeding of Fields

Fields seems like a simple subject, but many people get tripped up trying to implement them. Here are a few tips about fields to reduce your learning time.

❏ Create separate fields for first names and last names. Entering both names in the same field creates problems when you try to search and sort later. (We'll discuss sorting and searching in Chapter 7, *Searching Through Your Data* and Chapter 8, *Sorting Your Data*.)

❏ Create a separate field for social titles ("Mr.," "Ms.," "Dr."). Entering social titles in the First Name field makes the "Mr.'s" appear together when you sort by first name, potentially introducing error into the alphabetical order. For example, you could end up with the kind of sort that follows. (More on social titles in the next chapter.)

Bob

Greg

Lenny

Mr. Guy

Mr. Steve

Mr. Tom

Nancy

Oliver

❏ Vary the data, not the fields. Suppose that you keep track of customers, vendors, and friends. You might be tempted to create a Customer field, a Vendor field, and a Friend field. Instead, create a field called Category where you enter the text "customer," "vendor," or "friend." You'll use fewer fields and find information much more easily this way.

❑ Use more fields rather than less. Many companies have addresses like "1500 Stevens Creek Blvd., Suite 1501." It's better to put "1500 Stevens Creek Blvd." in an Address 1 field and "Suite 1501" in an Address 2 field.

If you follow these tips, your fields will lead happier and more fulfilled lives. It took me a long time to learn these tips, so I hope you'll learn from my experiences.

Summary

Designing a database is an art because you design a structure to hold your information. Like every good artist, you must be willing to throw away your first few attempts.

Quiz

1. The first name and last name of a person should not be in the same field. Why?

   ❑ It's sexist

   ❑ It produces problems when searching and sorting

   ❑ In California, first names and last names need their own space

2. What will happen if you store ZIP codes in a number field?

   ❑ Your mail will take longer

   ❑ East coast ZIP codes (that is, the ones that begin with "0") will get fouled up

   ❑ You'll look like a bozo if a knowledgeable database user sees this

3. What's wrong with this mailing label? How could you prevent the problem?

Joe Shmoe
14650 Stevens Creek Blvd., Suit
Cupertino, CA 94321

❏ Format ZIP codes: "950145505" becomes "95014-5505."

Automatic formatting is a handy feature of many Macintosh databases. It can make data entry faster and easier.

Duplicating Records

Sometimes you have to enter several people who work at the same company—for example, when you return from a trade show where you met several people from Apple in Cupertino. Their addresses are all 20525 Mariani Ave., Cupertino, CA 95014. Only their telephone numbers and mail stops are different.

Most databases enable you to duplicate records. This means that the record is copied, so you need to type only the information that is different. Often you only need to change the first name and last name information.

Saving and Entering

When you have finished typing the information into a record, you save the record. (This is also called entering the record.) You do this with most database products by pressing the Enter key or the Return key.

This is the consummate act of data entry; it signifies that you have finished with the record and want to move on to the next record or some other database function. Always remember: tab within a record and save (or enter) between records.

Data Entry Insights

I've entered a lot of records in my time, and I've seen many people's databases. Let me shorten your data entry learning curve with four insights.

❑ Abbreviate names and addresses whenever you can. For example, "Acme Brush Co." is better than "Acme Brush Company." When you print labels, long names and addresses may not fit, and you don't want to shorten them right before a mailing deadline.

❑ Pick standard ways to enter data and stick with it. Entering a state as "Pennsylvania," "Penn.," and "PA" is going to create problems later when you want to find everyone who lives in Pennsylvania.

❑ Assume that you'll forget things, so enter more information than you think you'll need. You may be tempted to leave off the telephone area code of a frequently called number. Six months from now, though, you won't be able to remember if Yakima, Washington is 209 or 206.

❑ Consider ignoring people's social titles ("Mr.," "Ms.," "Dr."). Often social titles get you into more trouble than they are worth. A "Miss" can become a "Mrs." A "Mrs." becomes a "Ms." A "Dr." may get insulted by being addressed as "Mr."

By observing these practices, you'll probably save a great deal of time and prevent a great deal of aggravation as you use your database.

There Are Better Ways

There are two more ways to enter data into your database. First, you can import data from another source such as another software program. We'll cover this subject in Chapter 10, *Exchanging Information*.

Second, you can obtain a data file from someone that already has information in it. For example, I have a database that contains press, developer, consultant, Apple employee, analyst, and retailer contacts in the Macintosh industry. You could use this as a starting point and enter your own contacts.

Summary

Data entry is an unavoidable pain. If you're starting from scratch, enter records as you need them. If you're lucky, you may be able to import existing information or get someone else's data file.

Quiz

1. Data entry is a _____

2. The definition of tabbing is

   ❏ Paying for the drinks of others

   ❏ Moving from field to field by pressing the tab key

3. Which is an example of a social title?

   ❏ Mr.

   ❏ Bozo

   ❏ Programmer

   ❏ Marketer

ZIP, and phone numbers. Figure 5–1 is an example of a detail view.

Figure 5–1 TouchBASE detail view

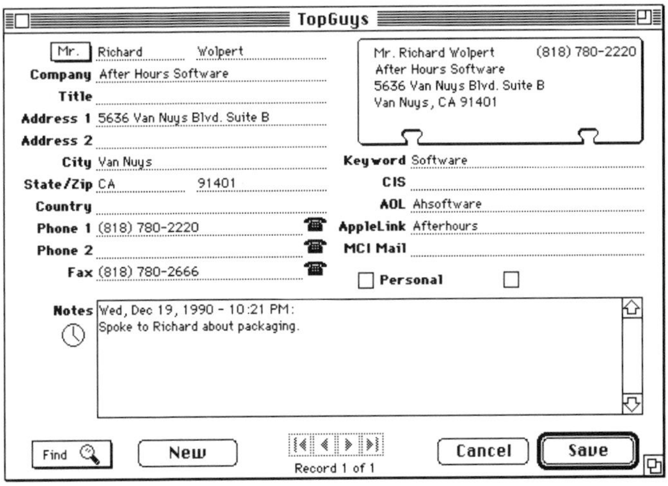

Looking at a detail view is analogous to looking at one information sheet inside of a binder. The purpose of this view is to provide as much information as possible for one record.

The List View

The second kind of view shows you many records at a time but less information about each record. This is the list view. The list view looks like the rows-and-columns format of a spreadsheet.

The list view serves two purposes: first, it enables you to scan many records in a short time. Second, it provides, at a glance, the information that you most often need (for example, a phone number).

Most databases enable you to select which fields you see in the list view. Usually, you select the fields that you need to see most often such as First Name, Last Name, Company, and Phone. Figure 5–2 is an example of a list view.

Figure 5–2 TouchBASE list view

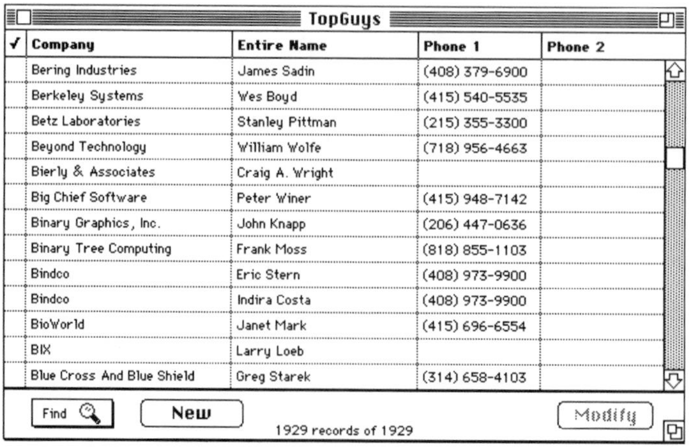
TopGuys

✓	Company	Entire Name	Phone 1	Phone 2
	Bering Industries	James Sadin	(408) 379-6900	
	Berkeley Systems	Wes Boyd	(415) 540-5535	
	Betz Laboratories	Stanley Pittman	(215) 355-3300	
	Beyond Technology	William Wolfe	(718) 956-4663	
	Bierly & Associates	Craig A. Wright		
	Big Chief Software	Peter Winer	(415) 948-7142	
	Binary Graphics, Inc.	John Knapp	(206) 447-0636	
	Binary Tree Computing	Frank Moss	(818) 855-1103	
	Bindco	Eric Stern	(408) 973-9900	
	Bindco	Indira Costa	(408) 973-9900	
	BioWorld	Janet Mark	(415) 696-6554	
	BIX	Larry Loeb		
	Blue Cross And Blue Shield	Greg Starek	(314) 658-4103	

Find New Modify
1929 records of 1929

The absence of a list view in some databases forces you to look at your records one at a time—analogous to "leafing" through pages. This is pretty frustrating because it makes looking through your database a slow process. Never buy a database that doesn't provide a list view.

Using the Detail and List Views

Let's see how to use the detail and list views of your data. Suppose that we want to call John Sculley at Apple to make sure he builds a lightweight laptop. Using the list view, we can see about 20 records but only the first name, last name, company, and phone number of the records.

We scroll through the list (don't worry, we'll discuss more efficient ways to find individual records in Chapter 7,

Searching Through Your Data) until we see John's record. All we want is John's phone number, so the list view provides as much information as we need.

We call him, and, of course, we don't get past his secretary, so we decide to send him a fax. The list view doesn't show his fax number, so we double-click on his record and go to the detail view. This enables you to see more information than the limited list view—including John Sculley's fax number. Then we skip off to our fax machine and send him a fax.

Current Selection

An important concept in viewing data is the current selection of records. It refers to the records that you are currently using. The current selection can be all the records in your database or a subset of all the records in your database. For example, a subset of your database may be the people who live in California.

Returning to the binder analogy, suppose that the binder contained 1,000 information sheets. When you are using the entire binder, then the current selection is 1,000 sheets. If you pull out and use only five sheets, then the current selection is five sheets.

Understanding the concept of a current selection is crucial to using a database well because you perform many operations such as sorting, printing, exporting, and searching based on the current selection.

Summary

Databases provide detail and list views to enable you to see the contacts in your database. The current selection is the set of records that you are currently using.

Quiz

1. The detail view is analogous to looking at one information sheet.

   ❏ True

   ❏ False

2. A detail view provides more information than the list view.

   ❏ More

   ❏ Less

3. Which is the principal advantage of the list view?

   ❏ Shows more information about each person

   ❏ Shows more records at once

Nothing succeeds like address.

Fran Lebowitz

Navigating Through Your Data

Key concepts

■ Scrolling

■ Navigation buttons

Introduction

This chapter explains how to navigate through your database. After reading it, you should understand how to move between the records in your database.

Scrolling

In the previous chapter, we scrolled to find John Sculley's record. This term may not be familiar to you. Scrolling is computerese for the process of rolling information past your eyeballs. Information that is scrolling looks like the credits at the end of the movies.

(If you're like me, you never stay to watch movie credits, so this may not be an informative analogy. Of course, if you're like me, the credits of the movies you see aren't worth watching.)

To make your records scroll, most databases require you to hold down the mouse button while the pointer is on either the up or down scroll bar arrow. If you don't want the "credits" to scroll continuously, you can click above or below the elevator, and you move a screenful of records at a time. Figure 6–1 is an illustration of a pointer in a scroll bar arrow which causes downward scrolling.

Figure 6–1 Clicking in the scroll bar arrow to scroll down records

Phone 1	Phone 2
(415) 365-1919	
(415) 328-9181	
(617) 266-0148	
(818) 894-5799	
(408) 733-0745	
(206) 453-2729	
(213) 338-5738	
(415) 358-8600	

Phone 1	Phone 2
(415) 328-9181	
(617) 266-0148	
(818) 894-5799	
(408) 733-0745	
(206) 453-2729	
(213) 338-5738	
(415) 358-8600	

Scrolling is a simple way to search through your database. It's not as efficient as the searching techniques we'll discuss later, but it does work in cases when you haven't explicitly stored searchable information in your database. Let me explain.

Suppose that you want to create a list of people to invite to a party. Although you've kept track of names, addresses, and telephone numbers, you did not record which ones you'd invite to a party. (It probably never occurred to you to keep track of a strange thing like this.)

A good way to create this list is to scroll through your database to decide on a person-by-person basis: "She's a good customer." "He really helped me as a vendor." "He invited me to his party; I guess I have to invite him to mine." This is an example of how to use scrolling.

Navigation Buttons

Look at the detail view shown in Figure 6–2. See the arrow buttons along the middle of the bottom edge? These buttons are another way to navigate through your database. They take you from the record that you're looking at to the first, last, next, and previous records.

Figure 6–2 Navigating through records

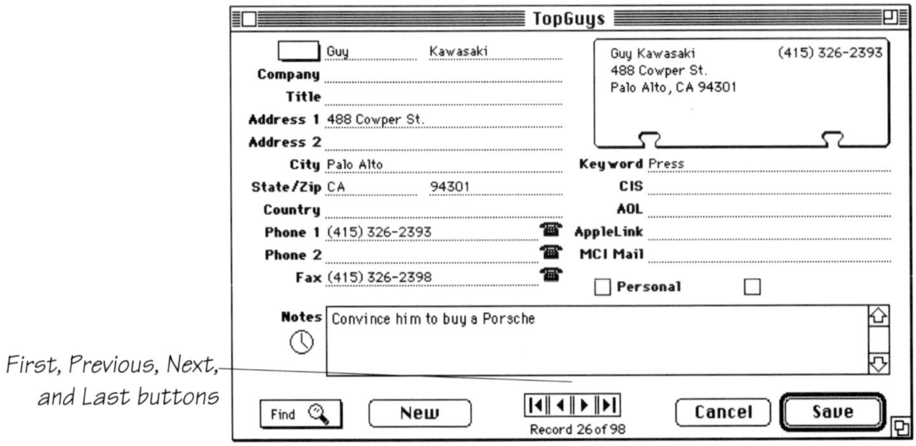

First, Previous, Next, and Last buttons

The Next and Previous buttons are useful for looking at records that are near the current record. For example, if you had alphabetized your records by company name, you might want to look at the other people who work for the same company.

The First and Last buttons take you to the first and last records in your database. I'm not convinced of the usefulness of the First and Last buttons because I've seldom had a burning need to move to the first or last record. Still, they look cool.

Summary

Scrolling and navigation buttons are two ways to move through your database. They sure beat flipping through pages in a binder.

Quiz

1. Your database has three records sorted in the following order.

   Kathy

   John

   Ted

   If you are looking at the detail view of John's record, which record will you see if you click on the Next button?

2. The purpose of navigation buttons is to

   ❏ Move between records

   ❏ Make your database look pretty

   ❏ Fill up your computer screen

3. Scrolling is

   ❏ Walking with a loved one through a park

   ❏ Photocopying religious documents

   ❏ Moving through the records of a database

> *Well, if I called the wrong number, why did you answer the phone?*
>
> James Thurber

Searching Through Your Data

Key concepts

- Strings

- Case sensitivity

- Multiple-condition searches

- Indexes

Introduction

This chapter explains searching. After reading it, you should understand fast and accurate ways to find information in your database. This is the longest chapter in the book because it covers one of the most important aspects of using a database.

Hunting for Treasure

Searching for information, assuming that you find it, is one of the three most rewarding aspects of owning a database. (The other two are printing labels and successfully merging with a word processor to create personalized letters.)

Finding the little nuggets of information that you entered is fun—it's like looking for treasure that you know is in the database (because you put it there) or like going trick-or-treating in a wealthy neighborhood. With databases, however, there are no "tricks." If you entered information, you will find it.

Without making a big deal about it, we discussed one kind of search in the previous chapter: scrolling through your database to search visually. This method, though useful in some cases, is too slow and imprecise for most searches.

What Is It?

When you search through a database, you need to know two things about your information: what is it and where is it.

What you're looking for is usually a name like "Smith," a company like "Apple," or a city like "Palo Alto." The name,

company, or city—that is, the value that you're looking for is called a string.

When most databases search for a string, they are not case sensitive. (Case sensitivity means that uppercase and lowercase letters are treated differently.) Thus, searching for the string "jud" or the string "Jud" is the same to a database. This means that you don't have to be as careful when you type in the search string.

There are varying degrees of "knowing" what you're looking for, and good databases anticipate this with different types of searches.

Begins With Search

A "begins with" search finds any record that starts with a string. For example, if you're not sure whether you entered

Apple Computer, Inc. as "Apple," "Apple Computer," or "Apple Computers, Inc.," then you do a "begins with" search for "Apple." Your database would find the company names that begin with "Apple" including Apple, Apple Computer, Appleton Hardware, and Apple Records.

A "begins with" search usually finds more records than you intended—Appleton Hardware and Apple Records, for example, in the search we just discussed. Nevertheless, this kind of search is useful when you're only sure of the first few letters of the information. You'll probably find yourself using a "begins with" search most of the time.

Exact Match Search

When you know *exactly* what you're looking for—right down to the last letter, space, period, tilde, accent, and umlaut—you use an "exact match" search. Exact means exact: if you do an "exact match" search for "Claris Corporation" and your data is actually "Claris" or "Claris Corp.," you're out of luck.

An "exact match" search, however, is useful for two reasons. First, an "exact match" search is efficient. It finds the fewest number of records. Second, an "exact match" search is usually faster. Usually, the more precise the string that you provide, the faster the database can perform the search.

Contains Search

When you know a few letters somewhere in the field, use a "contains" search. (If you knew it exactly, you'd use an "exact match" search. If you knew at least what it starts with, you'd use a "begins with" search.)

Suppose that you are looking in your database for a company named "Avalon Technology," but you can't remember "Avalon" as the first word. It may be "Abaton,"

"Micron," "Advanced," or "Emron," but you do remember that "Technology" is in the name.

In this case, a "contains" search for "technology" finds the records that contains the word "technology." Thus, you would find the records for "Avalon Technology" as well as "Abaton Technology," "Technology Works," and "*High-Technology Magazine.*"

A "contains" search is almost always the slowest type of search because it is the least precise, so your database must do a lot of work. Therefore, use it sparingly.

Where Is It?

In addition to knowing what you're searching for, you need to know where to search. In database vernacular, this means knowing which fields to look through. As you would expect, the more you can narrow down the places to look, the faster you'll find what you're looking for.

When You Know Which Field

When you know which field contains the information, then it's most efficient to search through only that field. For example, if you know that you want to find the people whose last name is "Kawasaki," you'd search only in the Last Name field and avoid wasting time looking through other fields.

Figure 7–1 is an example of searching through the Last Name field for last names that begin with "Kawasaki."

If there are any people's last names that begin with the string "Kawasaki," the database finds them. On the other hand, if there are people who work for Kawasaki Motorcycle Company, this search would not find them.

Figure 7–1 TouchBASE Last Name search screen

```
┌─────────────────────────────────────────────────────┐
│  ┌──┐  Enter the Last Name to search for...          │
│  │📄│                                                 │
│  └──┘                                                 │
│   ┌─────────────────────────────────────────────┐    │
│   │ Kawasaki                                     │    │
│   └─────────────────────────────────────────────┘    │
│  ┌─Search type:────────┐  ┌─List:──────────────┐     │
│  │  ● Begins With       │  │  ● Create New       │    │
│  │  ○ Exact Match       │  │  ○ Search Within    │    │
│  │  ○ Contains          │  │  ○ Append           │    │
│  └──────────────────────┘  └─────────────────────┘    │
│                                                       │
│                  ┌──────────┐  ┌──────────┐           │
│                  │  Cancel  │  │   Find   │           │
│                  └──────────┘  └──────────┘           │
└─────────────────────────────────────────────────────┘
```

When You Don't Know Which Field

Suppose that you're looking for someone you met a while ago, and you can't exactly remember his name. However, you recall that the name "Kawasaki" was somehow associated with his record as something to do with his last name or company name.

Figure 7–2 is an example of how to search through more than one field in this kind of situation.

Figure 7–2 TouchBASE search screen

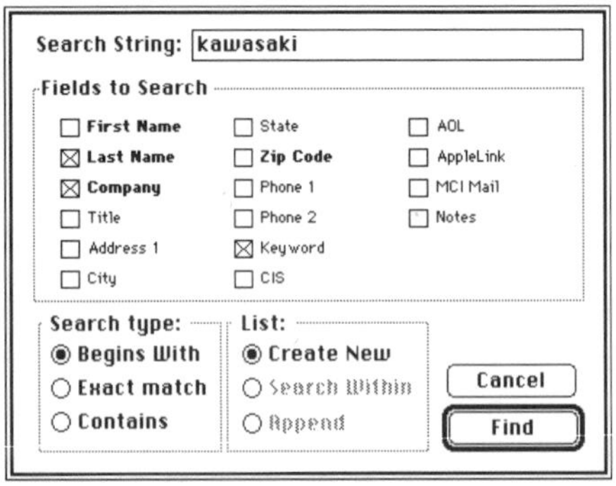

```
┌─────────────────────────────────────────────────────┐
│  Search String: ┌──────────────────────────────┐     │
│                 │ kawasaki                     │     │
│                 └──────────────────────────────┘     │
│  ┌─Fields to Search──────────────────────────────┐   │
│  │  ☐ First Name   ☐ State       ☐ AOL           │   │
│  │  ☒ Last Name    ☐ Zip Code    ☐ AppleLink     │   │
│  │  ☒ Company      ☐ Phone 1     ☐ MCI Mail      │   │
│  │  ☐ Title        ☐ Phone 2     ☐ Notes         │   │
│  │  ☐ Address 1    ☒ Keyword                      │   │
│  │  ☐ City         ☐ CIS                          │   │
│  └────────────────────────────────────────────────┘   │
│  ┌─Search type:──┐ ┌─List:────────┐                   │
│  │ ● Begins With  │ │ ● Create New  │  ┌──────────┐    │
│  │ ○ Exact match  │ │ ○ Search Within│ │  Cancel  │   │
│  │ ○ Contains     │ │ ○ Append      │  └──────────┘    │
│  └────────────────┘ └───────────────┘  ┌──────────┐    │
│                                         │   Find   │    │
│                                         └──────────┘    │
└─────────────────────────────────────────────────────┘
```

The database finds the records of anyone whose last name or company begins with the string "Kawasaki." Thus, it finds

"Guy Kawasaki" as well as "Kawasaki Motorcycle Company."

Multiple-condition Searching

The best way to explain multiple-condition searches is with a few examples. Suppose that you are trying to find someone in your database whose first name is John and who works at Apple. A single-condition search is "first name equals John." Unfortunately you have many people in your database named John so this search finds more records than you want.

Adding a second condition improves the precision of your search. The search would become "first name equals John" *and* "company equals Apple Computer, Inc." Your database finds fewer extraneous records since records must fulfill two search criteria.

There are two kinds of multiple-condition searches.

And Searches

The "first name is John and works for Apple Computer, Inc." search is an "and" multiple-condition search. This means that a successful candidate must fulfill more than one condition—like my wife telling me to wash the clothes *and* make dinner. As you can tell, multiple-condition "and" tasks are difficult and time-consuming.

Or Searches

The second kind of multiple-condition search is an "or" search. "And" searches find few records because two or more conditions must be fulfilled. "Or" searches find many records because only one of two or more conditions must be fulfilled. This is like my wife telling me to wash the clothes *or* make dinner *or* take out the garbage. Clearly, this is a lot easier to fulfill than doing all three chores.

Making Searches Faster

When you look for a book in the library, you can search through the shelves in a sequential manner. This method, however, is slow in a large library. A better method is to look up the book in the card catalog.

A card catalog contains indexes. Librarians created an index for each book according to name, author, and subject so that you won't have to search through the shelves of books.

Databases also create indexes so they don't have to search through each record sequentially. Typically, you index the fields that you'll most often search. In a contacts database, for example, you most frequently search the Last Name, First Name, and Company fields, so these are the most likely to index.

Why not index every field? There are two reasons. Let's return to the library analogy. First, indexing a book or data takes time—a librarian has to fill out cards and file them before the book can be put on the shelf. Likewise, if you indexed every field, data entry takes longer because the database has to create more indexes while it saves the record.

Second, after a while a library's card catalog fills up and the library has to buy more card catalogs. In the same way, indexing too many fields uses up more storage space on your floppy or hard disk, and you'd have to buy more storage.

Summary

Searching through your database is like finding treasure.

The next time your spouse tells you to wash the clothes, and make dinner, and take out the garbage, try telling him or her to change the request to "or" conditions for faster results.

Quiz

1. A "begins with" search for "Gas" will find "Gassée," "Gasoline," and "Gastrointestinal."

   ❏ True

   ❏ False

2. A librarian creates an index in order to

   ❏ Make finding books faster and easier

   ❏ Create employment

   ❏ Fill up the card catalog

3. A database creates an index in order to

   ❏ Make finding records faster and easier

   ❏ Use up disk space

   ❏ Make data entry slower

> *I hate housework! You make the beds, you do the dishes—and six months later you have to start all over again.*
>
> Joan Rivers

Sorting Your Data

Key concepts

- Ascending sorts

- Descending sorts

- Multiple-level sorts

Introduction

This chapter explains sorting. After reading it, you should understand how to alphabetize and rank the information in your database.

What Does Sorting Mean?

Though my wife disputes this, I cherish orderliness. (If you saw how I wash, fold, and put away the laundry, you would probably agree with her.) Sorting means ranking the data in one or more fields according to alphabetical or numerical ordering systems. Sorting a database is an example of orderliness in computers.

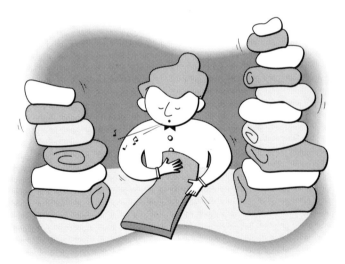

Ascending Sorts   An ascending sort means that your database ranks your data from A to Z. Figure 8–1 shows an example of sorting the Company field in a database in an ascending manner.

Figure 8–1 TouchBASE sorting by Company field

```
┌─────────────────────────────────┐
│  Sort Fields by...              │
│  ───────────                    │
│                                 │
│    Field: [ Company      ▼ ]    │
│                                 │
│         ◉ Ascending             │
│         ○ Descending            │
│                                 │
│      ( Cancel ) (    OK    )    │
│                                 │
└─────────────────────────────────┘
```

For example, this is a list of company names that is not sorted:

Apple Computer, Inc.

Claris

After Hours Software

Microsoft

Radius, Inc.

After an ascending sort, the list looks like this:

After Hours Software

Apple Computer, Inc.

Claris

Microsoft

Radius, Inc.

Descending
Sorts

A descending sort is the opposite of an ascending sort. Rather than putting things in order from A to Z, a descending sort does it from Z to A. The same list of addresses looks like this after a descending sort:

Radius, Inc.

Microsoft

Claris

Apple Computer, Inc.

After Hours Software

When do people use a descending sort? One occasion is when you have a numeric field containing the amount of business that you do with customers. A descending sort on this field shows who gives you the most business.

A word about case sensitivity in sorting: when most databases search for records, they are not case sensitive. This is also true when most databases sort. Thus, "jud" and "JuD" sort in the same way.

Also, remember our discussion of indexes in Chapter 7, *Searching Through Your Data.* Indexes make searches go faster, and they also make sorts go faster. Think about it this way: it is easier to sort the index cards in a card catalog than the books themselves.

Sorting Text Fields

Sorting on records that contain only letters is straightforward alphabetization. There are, however, a few complications when you sort text fields that contain both numbers and letters.

Numbers Before Letters

First, let's go back to Chapter 3, *Designing a Database,* where we discussed the difference between numbers and text. Recall that an address like "12 El Camino" or a com-

DB101 Quiz

1. Which list is correctly sorted in ascending order?

   One by One, Inc.

   1 On 1 Videos

   11-7 Drugstores

   1 On 1 Videos

   One by One, Inc.

   11-7 Drugstores

   1 On 1 Videos

   11-7 Drugstores

   One by One, Inc.

2. In a descending sort, numbers come before letters.

   ❏ True

   ❏ False

3. In an ascending sort, would "Beth" or "beTH" come first?

❑ Beth

❑ beTH

❑ It doesn't matter because sorting is not case sensitive

> *I always say, keep a diary and someday it'll keep you.*
> *Mae West*

Printing with a Database

Key concepts

- Reports
- Detailed reports
- Listing reports
- Address books
- Envelopes
- Labels
- Fax cover sheets

Introduction

This chapter discusses printing with a database. After reading it, you should understand the printing functions of a database, and you should want to damn the typewriters and go full speed ahead.

What Is Printing

Printing is a fundamental task of databases. It's the way to get the information from your database onto paper. (You do remember what paper is, don't you? It's the stuff that computers were supposed to make obsolete.)

Database printing can be divided into two general types. First, databases print reports that present the information in your database to you on paper. Second, databases print envelopes, labels, and fax cover sheets. These kinds of printing do not *present* the information to you as much as they *transfer* it from your database to paper.

Reports

Reports have several advantages over data that's stored in a computer. They are more permanent, they present information in more sophisticated ways, and you can photocopy and distribute them to other people.

Detailed Reports

Before you go to meet with a person, you may want to print out his or her address and phone number. This kind of report is a detailed report because it provides all the details about a person. It may seem pretty simplistic, but don't underestimate its value for tasks like jotting instructions to an administrative aide. Figure 9–1 shows a detailed report.

Figure 9–1 TouchBASE detailed report with instructions

Figure 9-1

detailed report with handwriting

reduce to 64 percent.

DO print keyline

Listing Reports   A listing report looks like the list view. This is a row-and-column report that shows a lot of records down the page and information about each record across the page. Figure 9–2 provides an example of a listing report.

Figure 9–2 FileMaker Pro listing report

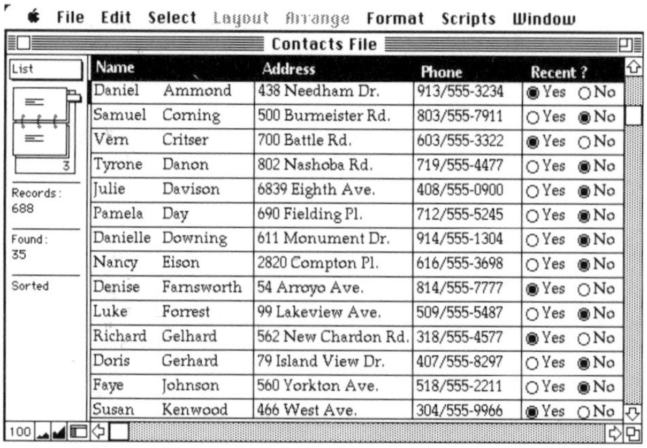

A listing report, like the list view, is useful to see information about a lot of people. For example, you would use a listing report to print out your customer list. Typically, an 8 ½-by-11-inch piece of paper can provide the name, company, address, and telephone number of about 75 people.

Figure 9–3 shows how to construct a listing report. You assemble your report by pointing and selecting the fields that you want to appear.

Another use of listing reports is to back up your database in case your computer fails or gets stolen. By printing out all your records, you have a paper version of your data that is impervious to floods, power outages, and computer viruses.

(I don't know why I mention this: most people never back up their data. Myself included.)

Figure 9–3 Creating a listing report with TouchBASE

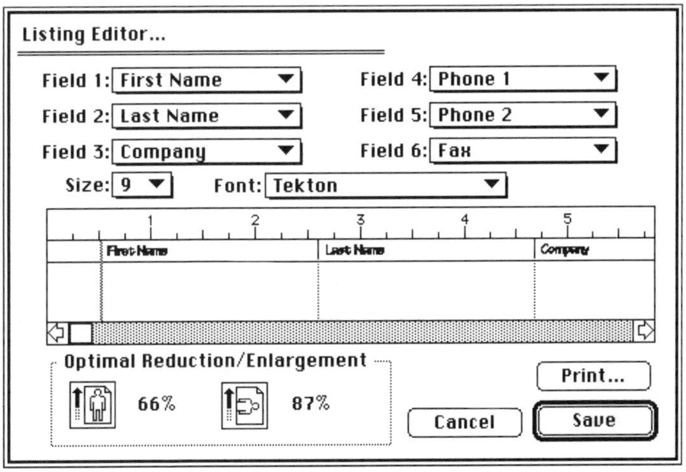

Address Books

If you ever picked up a Macintosh Portable, you know that it's a lot easier to carry an address book than a computer. ("Macintosh Portable" is an oxymoron as of the first half of 1991.) By printing address book format reports, you can access information when you are away from your Macintosh. Address book printing is simply a very specific type of report.

Databases make address books far easier to maintain and update. You keep your information in a database, and every once in a while you print it out. Between printings, you can make notes in your address book and then use the notes to update your database.

Envelopes, Labels, and Fax Cover Sheets

For the first five years of Macintosh's existence, printing envelopes and labels was a challenge. It seemed like no one at Apple thought about printing envelopes and labels. That's exactly what happened. When you're Steve Jobs (the chairman of Apple and general manager of the Macintosh Division) and you have two personal assistants, you don't think about printing an address on an envelope or a label.

When I worked at Apple, I had an area administrator named Carol Ballard, and she handled all this stuff for me. She—gasp—typed addresses with an IBM Selectric. I'd put her up against any database program, but there aren't many Carol Ballards in this world.

Thus, Macintosh owners had to send beautiful laser-printed letters in handwritten or typewritten envelopes for a long time. In this case, it never dawned on the shoemaker that his children needed shoes. It's a good thing that I quit Apple, or I would have never known either.

These printing problems changed recently when database companies realized that they should provide envelope and label printing capabilities as part of their product.

Envelopes

Now Macintosh databases can store your contacts' addresses and then print them onto envelopes. Some databases even print the postal bar code to speed up the delivery of your mail.

Figure 9–4 shows how to control the printing on an envelope. You select the size of the envelope, whether you want the return address and bar code to print, and how you are going to stick the envelope into your printer.

Figure 9–4 Printing an envelope with TouchBASE

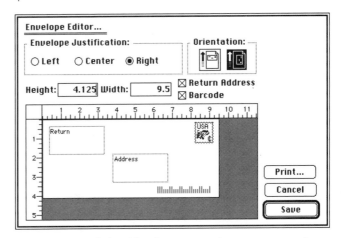

Printing capability like this means that even an underemployed author like me with no administrative assistant can send out beautifully addressed envelopes.

Labels

I love to print labels because it's satisfying to see 30 labels come out of the printer at a time. When you do a large mailing, labels are the only way to go.

Figure 9–5 illustrates how to select a label template. A template is a format that has been created for you by someone else, or that you create on your own. This one is for labels from Avery. Most database companies include templates of the most common labels so you don't have to design the templates yourself.

A well-designed database enables you to choose where the labels start printing, so that you can send a partially used sheet through the printer more than once. (You will also discover that most label sheets can't go through a printer more than three times because they curl up and jam the printer.)

Figure 9–5 Selecting a label template in TouchBASE

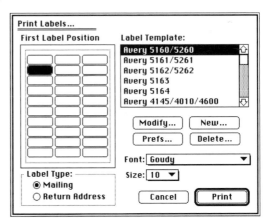

Figure 9–6 shows how to design a label template. By changing the number of rows and columns, the height and width of the labels, and the margins, you are able to accommodate any sheet of labels.

Figure 9–6 Designing a label template with TouchBASE

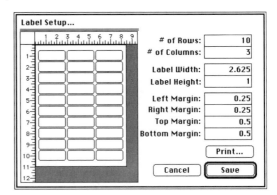

This screen also shows why you should buy a database with label templates. Trust me: you don't want to figure out these calculations—just buy the labels that match the templates.

Fax Cover Sheets At the beginning of the nineties, ugly fax cover sheets replaced handwritten envelopes. Most people use fax cover sheets that are a photocopy of a photocopy of a photocopy of a cover sheet that a clerk made three years ago on a typewriter.

A database changes this. With a database, you can find the person, get his fax number, and print a custom fax cover sheet with the person's name, fax number, and a message. Figure 9–7 shows how to create a fax cover sheet.

Figure 9–7 Creating a fax cover with TouchBASE

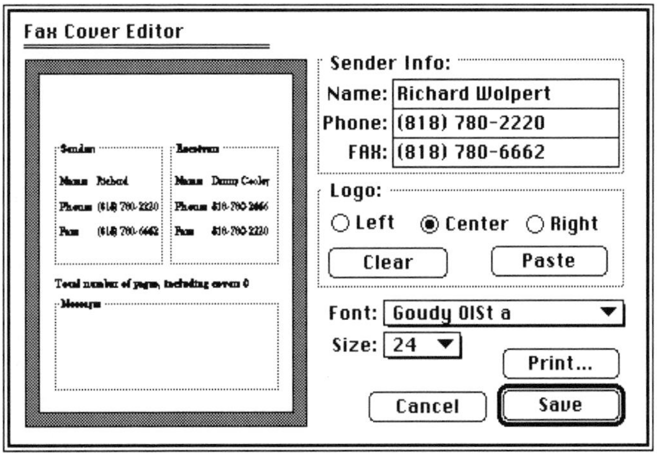

A database approach to printing cover sheets makes sending faxes more efficient and aesthetic. It doesn't quite justify buying a database, but what good is technology if you don't use it? By the way, I love to receive faxes, so if you like this book, send me a fax at 415-326-2398. (The fax number for negative comments is 415-555-1212.)

Summary

Printing is a fundamental function of databases. Reports present information. Envelopes, labels, and fax cover sheets transfer information. Now everyone can have as beautiful an envelope as a letter.

Quiz

1. Why haven't computers made paper obsolete?

   ❑ Paper is a convenient medium after all

   ❑ PostScript

   ❑ Paper lobbyists

2. Why weren't there good envelope and label printing products for Macintosh?

   ❑ Macintosh owners only played games

   ❑ Macintosh owners were attached to their Selectric typewriters

   ❑ Steve Jobs

   ❑ Carol Ballard

3. Why is "Macintosh Portable" an oxymoron?

   ❑ Size

   ❑ Weight

   ❑ Cost

   ❑ All of the above

> *I just put my feet in the air and move them around.*
> *Fred Astaire*

Exchanging Information

Key concepts

- Importing

- Exporting

- Delimiters

- Merging

Introduction

This chapter explains exchanging information. After reading it, you should understand transferring information between your database and other software programs.

The Top Ten Reasons to Use a Macintosh

Why do people use a Macintosh? Was it the cool thing to do? Did your company force you? Did you have $5000 burning a hole in your pocket? These are the top 10 reasons to buy a Macintosh.

10. You want to help pay for the Apple Christmas parties.

9. You hear that Apple provides great technical support.

8. Macintosh is a corporate standard so you have no choice.

7. You think that Macintosh has more software than Windows.

6. You think that you aren't buying a Macintosh but an IBM PC clone running Windows.

5. You want to design a car with a rotor on the roof.

4. You already have a yellow tie, condo, MBA, and espresso machine.

3. It is close to year end, and you need a tax deduction.

2. You want to transfer data from one program to another.

1. Macintosh is the only computer that you enjoy using.

One of the best reasons to buy a Macintosh is that you can easily and quickly transfer information between programs. Reason #2—the ability of Macintosh databases to exchange data with other programs—is the topic of this chapter. (To tell you the truth, transferring information is easy on all personal computers. I'm just biased.)

Importing into Your Database

Back in Chapter 4, *Entering Data,* we learned that data entry is a pain. There is a better way to get your information into a database than typing it from existing information. It comes, however, with one huge caveat: that the information is already in another program such as a spreadsheet, word processor, or even another database.

In these cases, transferring your information from one product to your database is easy: you export your information from one program and then import your data into your new database.

In some cases, importing is even liberating: for example, exporting your data from an IBM PC and importing it into a Macintosh.

This is how the process of importing data works.

❏ Select the records to export from the other program. In most cases, you'll be making a one-time conversion from one product to another, so you'll select all your records. You can also search for specific records and export just part of your database.

❏ Pick which fields to export. When you are converting from one product to another, you may not want to take all the information with you. For example, you may have kept track of birthdays, but you've found that you never send out cards anyway, so you don't want to retain this information.

❏ Choose the delimiters for fields and records. A delimiter is like a traffic signal for your database. When the information in the First Name field has been received, a delimiter tells your database, "Okay, that's all for the first name. Now let's bring in the last name."

When the entire record has been received, the delimiter tells your database, "Okay, that's the end of the record. Let's start the next one." Most databases use tabs and carriage returns as delimiters—that is, when your database sees a tab, it knows that a field has ended, and when it sees a carriage return, it knows a record has ended.

❏ Choose the fields in your database to import the information into. If your export file contains the First Name, Last Name, Company, Address 1, Address 2, City, State, ZIP, Phone, and Fax fields, then you import this information in the corresponding fields in your database. Figure 10–1 illustrates how to ensure that the fields match.

Figure 10–1 Matching fields in FileMaker Pro

Specify field order for import

Data In: "Export"   **Fields In: "Import"**

Data In: "Export"		Fields In: "Import"
First Name	→	First Name
Last Name	→	Last Name
Company	→	Company
Address 1	→	Address 1
Address 2	→	Address 2
City	→	City
State	→	State
Zip Code	→	Zip
Country	→	Phone 1
Phone 1	→	Phone 2
Phone 2	→	Country
Fax	→	Fax

《《 Scan Data 》》 Record 1   [Cancel]

◉ Add new records   [OK]
○ Replace data in current found set

Importing records saves a lot of time and effort compared to entering records by typing. Also, it reduces the amount of new errors and typos—or, it perpetuates the errors and typos that were in the original records.

Exporting from Your Database

Thus far we've considered importing data from other programs into your database. There are also times when you want to export information from your database to another program.

Here are some examples of reasons to export data from your database.

❑ You want to create personalized letters. These letters don't just say, "Dear Sir or Madam." They are individually addressed to people. This process is called merging. We'll discuss this process in the next section.

❑ You kept track of the members of your association in a database, and now you want to produce a membership directory, so you need to export your data and import it into a desktop-publishing program.

❑ You outgrew (or came to hate) your current database or IBM PC computer. Now you want to convert from one product to another without manually re-entering all the records.

Exporting from a database is the flip side of importing—that is, this time your database is doing the exporting not the importing. You select the records to export, pick the fields to export, choose the delimiters for the fields and records, and then export the data.

Merging

Merging refers to the process of combining information from more than one source. One common application of merging is combining the information from your database with a word-processing document to create personalized letters.

This is an overview of the process of merging names and addresses with a word processor.

❏ Select the records of the people to whom you want to send a letter from your database.

❏ Pick the fields that you want to export. (Typically the fields are First Name, Last Name, Company, Address 1, Address 2, City, State, and ZIP Code.)

❏ Export the records to a file.

❏ Create a letter with the names of the merged fields in your word processor. Figure 10–2 shows a MacWrite

II document with fields to merge. (The field names with the weird « and » symbols around them tells the word processor where to merge each field.)

Figure 10–2 MacWrite II document with merge fields

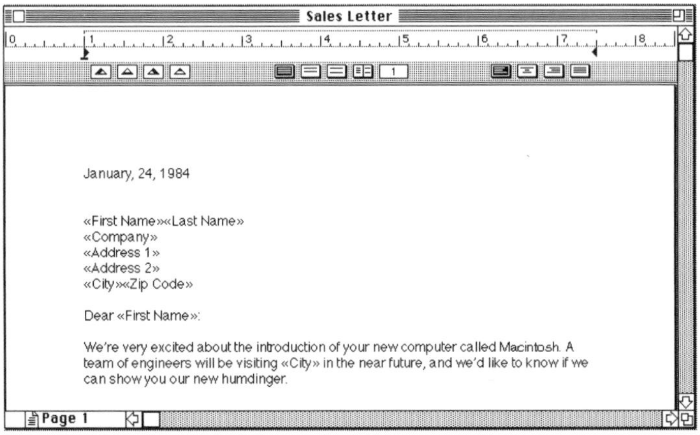

Sales Letter

```
10       1       2       3       4       5       6       7       8

January, 24, 1984

«First Name»«Last Name»
«Company»
«Address 1»
«Address 2»
«City»«Zip Code»

Dear «First Name»:

We're very excited about the introduction of your new computer called Macintosh. A
team of engineers will be visiting «City» in the near future, and we'd like to know if we
can show you our new humdinger.
```

Page 1

❏ Choose your word processor's merge option.

❏ Select the file that you exported from the database.

❏ Merge the file with your letter. Figure 10–3 shows how to begin the merging process in MacWrite II. Figure 10–4 shows the final result.

Figure 10–3 MacWrite II merge screen

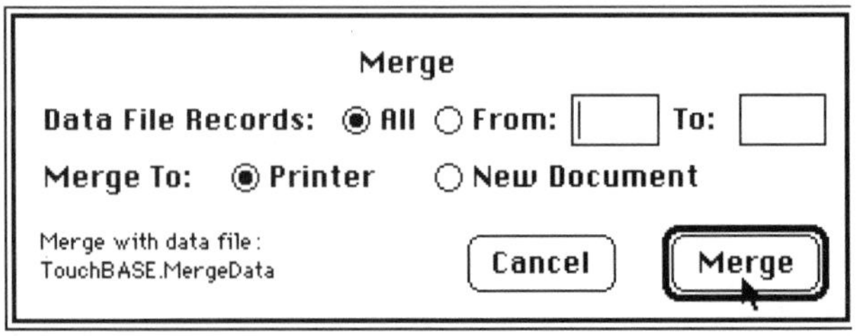

Merge

Data File Records: ● All ○ From: [   ] To: [   ]

Merge To: ● Printer   ○ New Document

Merge with data file:
TouchBASE.MergeData   [Cancel] [Merge]

Figure 10–4 The result of merging

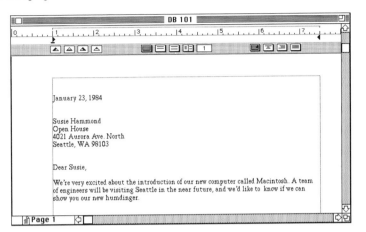

January 23, 1984

Susie Hammond
Open House
4021 Aurora Ave. North
Seattle, WA 98103

Dear Susie,

We're very excited about the introduction of our new computer called Macintosh. A team of engineers will be visiting Seattle in the near future, and we'd like to know if we can show you our new humdinger.

Copying a Record

Merging is a useful feature for creating more than two customized letters at a time. It is, however, overkill for creating one or two customized letters.

Suppose that you want to find one person in your database to get his name, company, and address for the address area in your word-processing document. You could retype all the information. This is crude, but it works. You could copy and paste each field into the word-processing document one at a time. This is crude, but it works. You could copy the entire record. This is cool, and it works.

Copying a record means that the database copies the information in several fields at once. (Typically, the fields are the First Name, Last Name, Company, Address 1, Address 2, City, State, and ZIP Code—that is, all the fields you need for the address area of a letter.) Then you could paste all this information into your letter at one time.

Summary

It's easy to transfer data from other programs to a database by exporting and importing. Merging information from a database into a word-processing document is particularly cool.

Quiz

1. Merging is

   ❑ The process of entering a freeway

   ❑ An analog act to continue the human race

   ❑ Combining data from different sources

   ❑ A Wall Street practice of combining two thriving companies to form a third that is less profitable

2. A delimiter is

   ❑ A signal that the end of a field or record has been reached

   ❑ A limit on the size of golden parachutes for Apple executives

   ❑ A see-through leather girdle used by Madonna

3. Why did you buy a Macintosh?

   ❑ I didn't; it was given to me as a gift

   ❑ I wanted to exchange data between programs

   ❑ I read *The Macintosh Way* and fell in love with the thought of owning a Macintosh

CHAPTER 11

> *Una bocca chiusa non prende mosche. (A closed mouth catches no flies.)*
>
> *Italian proverb*

Sharing Your Data

Key concepts

- Multi-user access

- File servers

Introduction

This chapter explains multi-user databases. After reading it, you should understand how people can share data over a network.

What's the Big Deal?

If you work in a company or office, multi-user access to a database is a big deal. Multi-user access means that more than one person can use the database at the same time.

You can think of a multi-user database as enabling more than one person to use a binder at the same time. Imagine that the information sheets are stored in a central binder, and people can look at sheets from their computers.

A multi-user database provides consistent and updated information to everyone using the database. This is very important, for example, when a customer moves and his address changes. If everyone had a separate database, then many separate database files would have to be updated. A multi-user database requires updating only one database file.

Multi-user Basics

Because of these advantages, multi-user databases are quite popular. In the simplest terms, this is how most multi-user databases work: you connect ("network" as computer gurus call it) all the Macintoshes together with wires.

There are two common kinds of wires: LocalTalk and Ethernet. LocalTalk is easier to install, slower, and cheaper. Ethernet is harder to install, faster, and more expensive.

VERSUS

Next you install a (legally obtained) copy of the database program on each Macintosh that needs to access the database file on the file server. Each person can access the database file from the Macintoshes on the network, and everyone lives happily ever after.

The Multi-user Rose Garden

That's the theory of multi-user databases. Now let me tell you the reality.

❑ Multi-user databases are ambitious projects. They require powerful hardware. They require connecting Macintoshes together. They may require hiring someone to manage the network.

❑ Multi-user databases are complex. It's a simple world when one person is using a database by himself. It gets tricky (when your mouth is open, flies go in) when several people are entering records, searching, sorting, and printing at the same time.

❑ Multi-user databases are usually slower. In a single-user database, data is on your local hard disk. In a multi-user database data has to flow through a wire and into your Macintosh. The wire is usually crowded because people are printing and sending messages over it at the same time that you're trying to access the database.

❑ Multi-user databases mean that "all the eggs are in one basket." If the database file is damaged, you can lose all your data. I'm sure that you diligently back up your database every night, but you won't have done so on the night that your database crashes.

Should your first database be multi-user? No way. It would be like learning to juggle with six balls. A multi-user database is too complex to be your first database.

Okay, if you don't want to listen to me, go ahead and buy a multi-user database. In the Macintosh world, you can pick from 4th Dimension, Omnis 5, Double Helix, TouchBASE, FileMaker Pro, and FoxBASE.

Summary

Multi-user databases are powerful and useful tools. They enable a group of people to share data and work more effectively. They are, however, ambitious projects not to be undertaken on a whim.

Quiz

1. What are the advantages of a multi-user database?

   ❏ Information is updated for everyone on the network

   ❏ You get to buy more powerful and expensive hardware

   ❏ You get to worry more since all your data is in one file

2. What are the disadvantages of a multi-user database?

   ❏ Information is updated for everyone on the network

   ❏ You get to buy more powerful and expensive hardware

   ❏ You get to worry more since all your data is in one file

3. A multi-user database can increase your risk if the database is damaged.

   ❏ True

   ❏ False

> I recoil, overcome with the glory of my rosy hue and the
> knowledge that I, a mere cock, have made the sun rise.
> Edmund Rostand

Personalizing Your Database

Key concepts

- Personalization

- Tab order

- Renaming fields

- Buttons

- Custom menus

Introduction

This chapter explains personalizing your database. After reading it, you should understand how to make your database work (more) the way you want it to be.

Personalization Defined

Personalization means customizing how your database works so that it is better suited to your needs. Personalization ranges from changing the tab order of fields to designing intricate layouts. Let's examine several ways to personalize a database.

Tab Order

Suppose that you seldom enter the addresses of people in your database because you primarily speak to people on the phone and seldom send them anything. During data entry, it's time-consuming to tab eight or nine times to get from the Company field to the Phone field. You'd rather tab directly.

Figure 12–1 shows how to change the tab order by creating a new sequence. The user would tab from First Name (#1) to Last Name (#2) to Company (#3) to Phone 1 (#4).

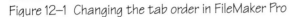

Figure 12–1 Changing the tab order in FileMaker Pro

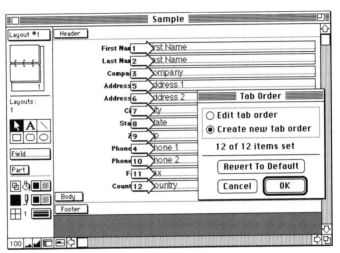

By changing the tab order, you can also skip over fields that you don't use and enter data much faster. For example, my database has a field for title and a field for country, but I seldom enter information in these fields. Hence, they are the last two fields in my tab order.

Renamed Fields

Another example of personalization is changing the names of fields. You might want to use a field to store birth dates or create a check box to record whether a person is married. (A check box is used for things that have only two states such as married or not.)

Figures 12–2 and 12–3 illustrate changing generic field names (Custom 1, Custom 2, etc.) to field names for specific purposes such as storing category type and electronic mail addresses.

Figure 12–2 TouchBASE detail view prior to renaming fields

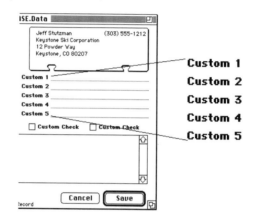

Figure 12–3 TouchBASE detail view after renaming fields

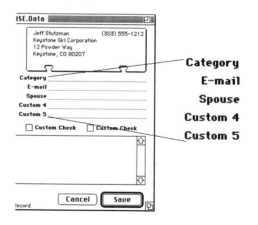

Buttons (and Bows)

In 1987 Apple introduced a program called HyperCard. It enabled people to create "stacks" of information. HyperCard changed the appearance of Macintosh software by introducing 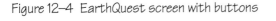 buttons that enabled people to point and click their way through stacks of information. Adding buttons is a third kind of personalization.

Figure 12–4 is a screen from a HyperCard stack called EarthQuest. By clicking on the buttons above the words "Planet," "Land," "Air," etc., you move to other screens in the database.

Figure 12–4 EarthQuest screen with buttons

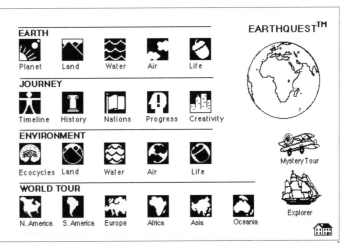

In the EarthQuest screen shown in Figure 12–5, users are able to click on the numbers and obtain more information about the toxics and garbage for each country.

Figure 12–5 EarthQuest screen with toxics and garbage buttons

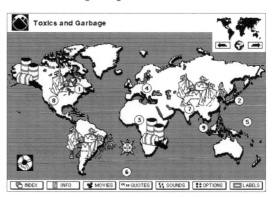

Database companies followed HyperCard's lead and enabled users to add buttons to their databases. These buttons help users move through records and other parts of their database with great ease.

Custom Menus

The final example of personalization is custom menus. Some databases allow you to create these pull-down menus and specify the functions that they perform. Figure 12–6, for example, shows a flight-planning database.

Figure 12–6 Flight-planning database by Will Mayall

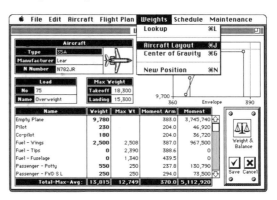

Personalization of this kind, like multi-user access, is a challenging and time-consuming task. Most database companies will tell you that you can point-and-click your way to custom menus. It isn't that easy, but the results can be spectacular.

Summary

Personalization is a way of changing your database so it works the way you want. It is a challenging process, but it can lead to important gains in productivity.

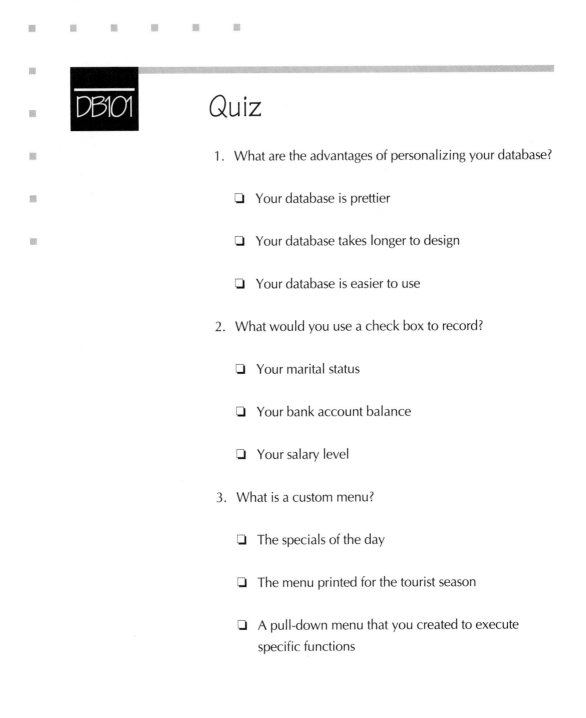

DB101   Quiz

1. What are the advantages of personalizing your database?

   ❏   Your database is prettier

   ❏   Your database takes longer to design

   ❏   Your database is easier to use

2. What would you use a check box to record?

   ❏   Your marital status

   ❏   Your bank account balance

   ❏   Your salary level

3. What is a custom menu?

   ❏   The specials of the day

   ❏   The menu printed for the tourist season

   ❏   A pull-down menu that you created to execute
        specific functions

> I recommend having no relationships except those easily
> borne and disposed of; I recommend limiting one's
> involvement in other people's lives to a pleasantly scant
> minimum.
>
> *Quentin Crisp*

Relational Databases

Key concepts

- The Relational model

- Flat-file databases

Introduction

This chapter explains relational databases. After reading it, you might understand relational databases in everyday, and perhaps theoretical, terms.

In Strict Terms

Relational databases are a tricky topic. Way back when, Dr. E. F. Codd formed "the Relational model" as a way to represent and manipulate data. His model bears little relevance to how you and I use a database on a day-to-day basis, so you might want to skip this section.

I'll try to explain Codd's Relational model as clearly and simply as I can. If you'd like to read more about the subject, I recommend a book called *Database: A Primer* by C. J. Date. Basically, Codd's Relational model centers on three things: data structure, data manipulation, and data integrity.

The data structure aspect of the model specifies that data should be represented in tables. A table is made up of a row of column headings with additional rows of data values. For example, this is a table.

People	Company
P1	C1
P2	C2
P3	C3

The data manipulation aspect of the model refers to a set of operators for manipulating the data in tables. Examples of operators are SELECT and JOIN. These operators do things like extract data and then combine it in different ways.

The data integrity aspect of the model requires that the database fulfill two rules. First, every table must have a primary key that uniquely identifies the records in the table. I barely understand the second rule, so I'll quote it from C. J. Date's book.

> *If table T2 includes a foreign key FK matching the primary key PK of table T1, then every value of FK in T2 must either (a) be equal to the value of PK in some record of T1, or (b) be null.*

The Relational model boils down to this: the reason relational databases are *relational* is because tables are a mathematical construct called a relation. Most people think that relational databases are called relational because files are "related" to each other—like parents and children. They are wrong, and now you know better.

In Practical Terms

Phew! That was a mouthful. (I told you to skip that section.) My editors tried to get me to cut the previous section, but I refused to just in case any "database scientists" read this book. I want them to know that I know what the term "relational database" really means.

Now I'm going to describe what almost everyone except Mr. Codd and Mr. Date and their relatives refer to as relational databases. You will probably decide to ignore The Relational model as well.

Remember the binder that contains information about your personal contacts? Let's call it the Contacts binder. The information sheets had fields like these below.

First Name

Last Name

Company Name

Address 1

Address 2

City

State

ZIP Code

Phone

Fax

This binder is a flat-file database because it is made up of only one file—that is, it has a flat structure. The shortcoming of a flat-file database is that information must often be stored repetitively; for example, if more than one person works for the same company at the same location, a flat-file database requires storing the company information more than once.

As Steve Jobs would say, "There must be a better way." There is. Imagine a second binder that contains one record for each company with its name, address, city, state, ZIP, phone, and fax information. Let's call it the Company binder.

When you add a new company to the Company binder, you create one new information sheet for it. When it moves or changes its phone number, you update one sheet. Now imagine that the Contacts binder can access all the company information that it needs from the Company binder.

Thus, if you were looking at John Sculley's record in the Contacts binder, Apple's name, address, city, state, ZIP, phone, and fax information comes from the Company binder.

If you looked at another person's record from Apple, his or her company information comes from the same record in the Company binder. When you updated Apple's address in the Company binder, the information update became available for every other record that refers to Apple.

Flat-file or Relational?

Learning to use a relational database comes at some cost: typically, relational databases are more expensive, and they take longer to learn. My advice is that you avoid a relational database at first. (Or, if you do buy a relational database, use it as a flat-file database until you're comfortable with it.)

Since relational databases are so powerful, they can quickly overwhelm you. If you're having trouble understanding databases, things can get worse if you buy a relational database. If you don't want to listen to me, then check out 4th Dimension, Double Helix, Omnis 5, and FoxBASE. They are all relational databases.

If you have trouble figuring out whether a database is flat or relational, here are two rules of thumb.

First, companies like to brag that their product is "relational." If it is, chances are that the company has emblazoned "RELATIONAL" all over the box and its ads.

Second, relational databases are more expensive. That's because they are harder to create, harder to explain to people how to use, and harder to convince you to spend more money on.

Summary

A relational database can save you a lot of work because it eliminates repetitive data entry and updating. I wouldn't buy one as a first database, but it is appropriate as you get more experienced with using a database.

Quiz

1. How many database files does a flat-file database contain?

   ❏ Two

   ❏ One

   ❏ None

2. The only person who should buy a relational database as his first database is a

   ❏ Masochist

   ❏ Hermit

   ❏ Genius

   ❏ Programmer

3. A relational database means you will have less repetitive data entry.

   ❏ True

   ❏ False

> *Not everything that is more difficult is more meritorious.*
> *Saint Thomas Aquinas*

Programming Languages

Key concept

 Programmability

Introduction

This chapter explains database programming languages. After reading it, you should understand the power and danger of a database programming language.

What Is a Database Programming Language?

A database programming language is a way to tell your database to perform certain functions. As a rule of thumb, a database programming language is about as sophisticated as the computer programming languages BASIC and Pascal.

A database programming language isn't necessary for all database users, but it can increase the functionality of a database. Here are examples of what a database programming language can do for you.

❑ Define and validate data such as limiting the ranges of salaries in a field and requiring that numbers, not letters, are entered in a Salary field.

❑ Perform complex reporting operations such as multiplying a price by a quantity to get a cost, adding all costs together, calculating sales tax, and then adding a shipping charge based on the total cost.

o Automate tasks such as capitalizing first letters of names, formatting telephone numbers, and formatting ZIP codes.

In each case, a database programming language adds to the functionality of a database—making it a more useful and versatile tool.

Do You Need One?

Do you need a database programming language? This is a good question. A database programming language can open up many additional functions, or it can drown you. Whether you need one is a difficult question to answer so Table 14–1 provides the pros and cons.

Unfortunately, the presence of a programming language often means that the database doesn't automatically handle tasks such as data validation and formatting. This in turn means that you may need to program these functions. As

Table 14–1 Pros and cons of database programming languages

Pro	Con
• Provides greater functionality and flexibility	• Increases learning time (if you use the programming language)
• Reduces the likelihood you will outgrow your database	• Probably comes in databases that are more expensive
	• Frequently means you need more RAM and a more powerful computer

Saint Thomas Aquinas would say just because this is more difficult, doesn't mean it's meritorious. Why should you have to program your database to format telephone numbers?

If you are buying your first database, I'd recommend one that doesn't contain a programming language. This is analogous to ski instructors telling you to buy short skis and set your bindings on a low tension so that you don't kill yourself.

Database Consultants

A programming language as well as multi-user, personalization, and relational capabilities are beyond the expertise of most novice database owners. Most people don't have the time, inclination, or knowledge to use these powerful features.

For these people, God invented consultants. They can be, however, a black hole for your money. Here's advice from a retired president of a database company on how to choose a database consultant.

❏ Call the database company for a referral. Usually these companies have "pet" consultants that they recommend. (If a company doesn't have pet consultants, you should think twice about using its products.) These consultants became pets because they know the product well (and they did a bit of brown-nosing).

❏ Like the old adage says, "You pay for what you get." As of this writing, a reasonable per hour fee for a good consultant is $100/hour and climbing in major cities. Use this as a rule of thumb. If a consultant quotes you something much lower, ask him how long he's been in business. If he quotes you something much higher, show him this paragraph.

❏ Unfortunately, the other half of the adage: "You get what you pay for," isn't always true. If you get taken, I have some sympathy for you, but it's probably your fault.

❏ More than anything else, the references of past clients should guide your selection of a consultant. Ask the prospective consultants for a list of references. Then ask the references about the consultant's quality of work, delivery schedule, and willingness to do updates and bug fixes. Then ask the $64,000 question: "Would you hire him again?"

Don't call the database company for a reference (as opposed to a referral). I doubt that they would tell you that one of their consultants is a bozo because database companies want all the consultants that they can get. They aren't going to risk you calling the consultant and saying, "The company told me you're a bozo."

Summary

A programming language can give you greater control over your database. This power, however, comes at considerable costs including learning time, the price of the database, and what kind of computer can run the database.

Quiz

1. Why would a company include a database programming language in its product?

   ❏ To increase its tech support calls

   ❏ To compensate for functionality it left out

   ❏ To provide greater power and flexibility to its customers

2. Which are reasons to want a database programming language?

   ❏ You are a tweak

   ❏ You have a lot of spare time

   ❏ You are a masochist

3. Which are reasons not to want a database programming language?

   ❏ You have a balanced life

   ❏ You are a passenger, not a sailor

   ❏ You have simple database needs

> We call a man a bigot or a slave of dogma because he is a thinker who has thought thoroughly and to a definite end.
>
> G. K. Chesterton

Databases for More Than One Kind of Computer

Key concepts

- Symmetry

- Yin and yang

- Poetic justice

- Multiple-platform databases

121
DB101

Introduction

This chapter explains the concept and reality of multiple-platform databases. After reading it, I hope you decide not to buy a multiple-platform database.

The Other Side of Personal Computing

Like eating gefilte fish or haggis, this chapter isn't for everyone. If it were up to me, this chapter would be irrelevant because everyone would use a Macintosh. If you believe in symmetry, yin and yang, and poetic justice, then you have to believe that there is another side to personal computing. The other side is the IBM PC and all its clones.

The IBM PC has its own selection of databases. They range from flat-file to relational, single-user to multi-user, and bozo to brilliant just like Macintosh databases. Companies with Macintoshes and IBM PCs need a database that can run on both the IBM PC and Macintosh. The computer trade calls these products multiple-platform databases. "Multiple" because the databases run on more than one kind of computer. "Platform" because platform is a fancy word for a type of computer.

The theory is that people will be able to use the same database whether they are using an IBM PC, Macintosh, or other kind of computer. This is especially seductive on a multi-user network so that people on different platforms (don't you just love this word?) can use the same information.

There are three multiple-platform Macintosh databases: FoxBASE, Omnis 5, and Double Helix. FoxBASE and Omnis 5 run on both the IBM PC and Macintosh. Double Helix runs on

DEC Vaxes and Macintosh. These products should make anyone who needs a multiple-platform database happy.

Should You Buy a Multiple-platform Database?

I doubt that multiple-platform capability is an important issue for most people who are reading this book. Anyway, there's something impure and suboptimal about multiple-platform databases. Let me explain.

Creating a computer is a personal and religious experience for engineers. It is an art for these people; it is not a production process. The people who created Macintosh were trying to revolutionize the world; their "guns" and "declarations" were Macintoshes and LaserWriters.

Using a Macintosh is like floating in clouds; using an IBM PC is like wallowing in mud. One database cannot take full advantage of the features of both computers. Thus, multiple-platform databases are written for the lowest common denominator and carry the baggage of the platforms they run on. End of sermon.

Summary

Companies often have more than one kind of personal computer in their offices. If you're in a company like this, you can either buy a multiple-platform database, make everyone switch to one kind of computer, or isolate yourself.

DB101

Quiz

1. Why would a company have more than one kind of computer?

   ❑ Bad luck

   ❑ The previous MIS (Management Information Services) administrator

   ❑ The previous purchasing agent had a relative at IBM

2. Do you consider yourself the kind of person who likes lowest common denominator products?

   ❑ Yes

   ❑ No

3. Where would you rather be?

   ❑ In the clouds

   ❑ In the mud

Do not use a hatchet to remove a fly from your friend's
forehead.

Chinese proverb

Buying
Your First
Database

Key concepts

- Be willing to throw away your first database

- Test driving

- Demo version

Introduction

This chapter explains the process of buying your first database. After reading it, you should put away your hatchet.

Basic Issues

Buying a database is a bewildering experience. Every company will tell you that its product is fast, easy to use, bug-free, and flexible. This isn't true. Every company will also tell you that its product is appropriate for your needs. This isn't true, either.

Under the best conditions, you're going to buy a database based on using a demo version, word-of-mouth recommendations, and reviews (listed in order of credibility) If you decide a few issues in advance, it will make your search a lot easier. Here are the three most important ones.

High-end Features

The first issue is what kind of high-end features you need. In previous chapters we've discussed multi-user access, relational capabilities, programming language, and multiple-platform availability. As I said, these high-end capabilities are probably overkill for most people's first databases.

Each of these features adds considerable power and flexibility, but each also makes learning and using a database harder. If you are sure you need these features, then buy a database with them. If you run into trouble, consider using a database consultant for help.

Quantity of Records

The second issue is the quantity of records that a database can realistically handle. The capacity of a database is determined by two factors: the kind of computer you're using and the design of the database. (What you *hear* as a database's capacity is determined by how much the database vendor is willing to stretch the truth.)

Table 16–1 provides approximate (and debatable) guidelines for how many records each model of Macintosh can handle. Additional RAM and faster hard disks can increase capacity, so I may be off by a factor of 50 percent. If anyone, however, tells you that I'm wrong by a factor of ten, watch his or her nose grow longer.

Table 16–1 The number of records each Macintosh can handle

Model	Number of records
Macintosh Plus	1,000
Macintosh Classic	1,500
Macintosh Portable	1,500
Macintosh SE	1,500
SE/30	5,000
Macintosh II	5,000
Macintosh IIcx	7,500
Macintosh IIci	15,000
Macintosh IIfx	25,000

Database vendors design their products with a practical limit of records in mind. They don't tell you what the number is, however, because they don't want to limit the market for their products or look bad in reviews.

My theory is that the suggested retail price of a database is a good guide to the capacity of a database. This is because database vendors price their products based on how power-ful and how much capacity they think their products have. Table 16–2 provides a guideline to the number of records a database can handle based on its price.

Be aware of the difference between "theoretical" limits and "practical" limits. All that matters is the practical limit—

that is, how many records can you expect to use in the real world. If you want to learn the practical limits, ask the vendor, "How many records would you tell your mother-in-law your product could handle?"

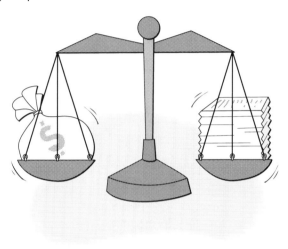

Table 16–2 The number of records a database can handle organized by price

Price	Number of records
Under $200	2,500
$200–400	5,000
$400–600	10,000
$600 plus	25,000

Speed Versus Ease of Use

The third issue is the tradeoff between speed and ease of use. (Many database vendors and gurus dispute that there is a tradeoff. They're wrong.) Generally, if you want a database that is fast, you have to put up with a more difficult product to use. If you want an easy-to-use database, you have to put up with a slower product.

The reason for this tradeoff is that the interface that makes a database easy to use—graphics, iconic representations, and multiple fonts—makes a computer work harder. Since it's working harder, other processes take longer—it's like turning on the air conditioning in a car when you're driving up a hill. Your car will go slower (but you will be more comfortable inside it).

This tradeoff is a very tricky issue, so don't go rushing off assuming that you know you want speed at all costs (or vice versa). There is "benchmark" speed and there is "throughput" speed. Some products excel at benchmark speed: this is when someone measures tasks like importing, exporting, searching, and sorting, and then reports the results in minutes and seconds.

Throughput speed is different. It is a product's performance when a normal human being is using the product. Suppose Product A imports records twice as fast as Product B. Product A, however, is harder to use so a person has to fiddle around a long time to set up importing. Product B imports slower but is easier to use. The user of Product B may finish importing before the user of Product A.

Let's return to the air conditioning analogy. Two cars set out for the same destination. One has air conditioning; the other doesn't. The one with air conditioning goes slower because it drains power from the engine. The driver of the car without air conditioning goes faster but gets exhausted by the heat so he has to make frequent rest stops. The slower car may get to the destination first.

It's difficult to decide the issue of speed versus ease of use in advance. It depends on how often you need to do each process, how much time you can spend learning to use your database, and how much you value your time. Thus, I propose the Kawasaki Database Purchase Algorithm.

The Kawasaki Database Purchase Algorithm

Back in Chapter 3, *Designing a Database,* I told you that you'll probably throw away the first two or three databases that you design. I hate to tell you, but you'll also probably throw away the first database—that is, the product itself— that you buy.

This is how I think you should try to find the database that's right for you. It's a simple four-step process that reflects the difficulty of finding the right database.

1. Buy a simple database.

2. Use it for a while.

3. Throw it away.

4. Buy the one you should have bought in the first place, had you known better.

This sounds cavalier and wasteful of your money, but you can believe me now or you can believe me later. Many people buy a second or third database. Like I said before, using a database is a process, not an event.

The Poor Man's Kawasaki Database Purchase Algorithm

Okay, so you don't want to take my advice. I'll give you a slightly less expensive way to start out. Buy the demo version of all the databases that you can find. Typically, these databases are limited in their capacity or their ability to print. They enable you to test drive a product before you buy it.

As I stated before, I've included a demo copy of TouchBASE and FileMaker Pro. They are limited in terms of the number of records that you can add to them but are otherwise fully functional. Instructions are in the appendix to help you install both demo versions on your computer.

Summary

Buying your first database should be a fun experience. Go out and ask your friends what they use, read all the reviews that you can, and get demo versions of the software.

DB101 Quiz

1. Did you marry the first person you dated?

   ❑ Yes

   ❑ No

   ❑ I'm not married

2. If you married the first person you dated, what happened?

   ❑ Remained happily married

   ❑ Got happily divorced

   ❑ It's still unclear

3. The demo version of a company's product is a powerful indication of the company's commitment to quality.

   ❑ True

   ❑ False

> *Abuse is often of service. There is nothing so danger-ous to an author as silence. His name, like the shuttle-cock, must be beat backward and forward, or it falls to the ground.*
>
> —Dr. Samuel Johnson

Conclusion

Review

If you've come this far, you've acquired a solid foundation of database knowledge. You should be able to discuss databases with most people and make a good choice when buying a database product.

Let's review what you've learned. We started out by defining what a database is and explaining files, records, and fields. Then you learned how a database can help you be more productive.

Next you learned about using databases—how to design a database, enter records, view information, search for records, sort records, and print envelopes, labels, fax cover sheets, and reports.

Next you learned about exchanging information between programs, and then we covered some high-end topics like sharing data on a network, personalizing a database, relational databases, programming languages, and multiple-platform databases.

Finally, you learned how to buy your first database by using the Kawasaki Database Purchase algorithms and you learned that you'll probably throw away your first database.

When all is said and done, just go out and have fun. Buy a database. Put your data into it. Print some envelopes and labels. Do a few merged letters to your friends. Have a blast—it's the Macintosh way.

Reach Out and Touch

Thank you very much for buying or reading this book. I hope that you've enjoyed it and that you learned a lot about databases.

If you have any comments about how to make it better (I will also accept unadulterated praise), please contact me in any of the following ways.

Guy Kawasaki
P.O. Box 146
Palo Alto, CA 94301

America Online: Mac Way
CompuServe: 76703,3031
AppleLink: Kawasaki2
Phone: 415-326-2393
Fax: 415-326-2398

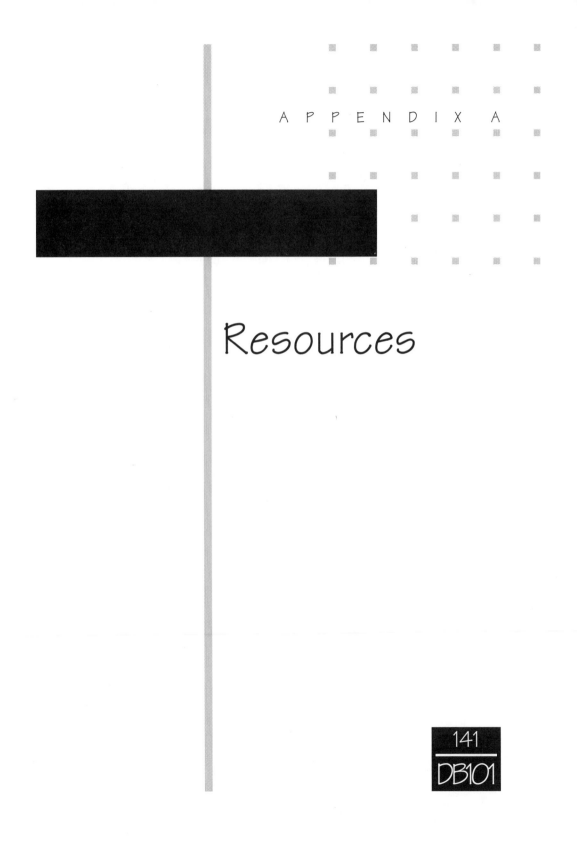

APPENDIX A

Resources

141
DB101

This appendix contains the names, addresses, and phone numbers of most of the Macintosh database companies.

ACIUS, Inc.
10351 Bubb Road
Cupertino, CA 95014
408-252-4444
Fax: 408-252-0831
Products: 4th Dimension and File Force

After Hours Software
5636 Van Nuys Boulevard, Suite B
Van Nuys, CA 91401
818-780-2220
Fax: 818-780-2226
Product: TouchBASE

Ashton-Tate
20101 Hamilton Avenue
Torrance, CA 90509
213-538-7350
Fax: 213-538-7996
Product: dBASE IV for the Mac

Blyth Software
1065 E. Hillsdale Boulevard
Foster City, CA 94404
415-571-0222
Fax: 415-571-1132
Product: Omnis 5

Claris Corporation
5201 Patrick Henry Drive
Santa Clara, CA 95052-8168
408-987-7000
Fax: 408-987-7105
Product: FileMaker Pro

Fox Software
118 W. South Boundary
Perrysburg, OH 43551
419-874-0162
Fax: 419-872-9514
Product: FoxBASE+/Mac

Odesta Corp.
4084 Commercial Avenue
Northbrook, IL 60062
312-498-5615
Fax: 312-498-9917
Product: Double Helix

Preferred Publishers, Inc.
1770 Moriah Woods Boulevard
Suite 14
Memphis, TN 38117-7118
901-683-3383
Fax: 901-683-4983
Product: DAtabase

ProVUE Development Corp.
1518 Transistor
Huntington Beach, CA 92649
714-892-8199
Fax: 714-893-4899
Product: Panorama

Software Discoveries, Inc.
137 Krawski Drive
South Windsor, CT 06074
203-872-1024
Fax: 203-644-2081
Product: RecordHolder Plus

How to Test Drive TouchBASE and FileMaker Pro

This appendix contains instructions on how to install and use the demo versions of TouchBASE and FileMaker Pro.

Getting Ready

The first step to test driving either TouchBASE and FileMaker Pro is to install the programs on your Macintosh. These instructions explain how to copy the "Database 101" file from the floppy disk to your hard disk and then decompress it. The file was compressed in order to make it everything fit on one disk.

1. Insert the disk into your Macintosh.

2. Copy the icon named "Database 101" to your hard disk.

3. Double-click on the Database 101 icon on your hard disk. (This decompresses the file and installs two folders—"TouchBASE Folder" and "FileMaker Pro Folder"—on your hard disk.)

FileMaker Pro

FileMaker Pro is a stand-alone program. All you have to do is double-click on its icon to launch it, and you can begin using it.

TouchBASE

TouchBASE is a desk accessory. To use it, you must install it in your System file. TouchBASE requires System 6.0.5 or better.

1. Copy the TouchBASE.Prefs file into your system folder.

2. Double click on the Font/DA Mover icon. The Font/
    DA Mover dialog box opens with the Font radio
    button selected and the list of fonts currently installed
    in your System file.

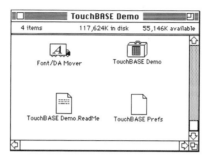

3. Click on the Desk Accessory radio button. The box on
    the left will now show the desk accessories currently
    installed in your System.

4. Click on the Open... button below the empty box on
    the right. A dialog box appears.

5. Select the TouchBASE Demo file in the TouchBASE
    Demo folder.

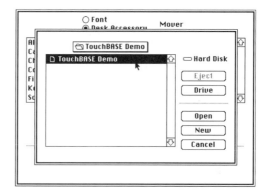

6. Click on the Open button. "TouchBASE Demo" should now appear in the right box of the Font/DA Mover dialog box.

7. Click on Copy. This installs "TouchBASE Demo" into your System file.

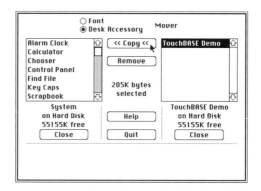

8. Click on the desk accessory menu (the one with the Apple icon) to launch TouchBASE. Restart your computer if TouchBASE doesn't appear, and then try launching TouchBASE again.

If you are using System 7.0, you can avoid Steps 2–7 by dragging the TouchBASE Demo file into the folder called Apple Menu Items in your system folder.

Index

This book was typeset in Adobe's version of Optima, with heads set in Tekton. It was produced by Open House using Aldus PageMaker, and imageset at Seattle ImageSetting.

More from Peachpit Press...

CANNED ART: CLIP ART FOR THE MACINTOSH
▲ *Erfert Fenton and Christine Morrissett*
A fully indexed sample book showing over 15,000 pieces of clip art available from 35 different companies. Includes tear-out coupons for over $1,000 in discounts on commercial clip art. The two optional All Star Sample Disks contain 61 pieces of clip art. *(825 pages)*

CANVAS 3.0: THE BOOK
▲ *Deke McClelland*
The first book on the popular Macintosh painting program from Deneba Systems. *(320 pp)*

HELP! THE ART OF COMPUTER TECHNICAL SUPPORT
▲ *Ralph Wilson*
The first practical guide on the subject of technical support. Explains how to set up and manage a tech support operation. *(260 pages)*

LEARNING POSTSCRIPT: A VISUAL APPROACH
▲ *Ross Smith*
An easy show-and-tell tutorial on the PostScript page description language. *(426 pages)*

THE LITTLE MAC BOOK, 2nd Edition
▲ *Robin Williams and Kay Nelson*
Peachpit's bestselling beginner's guide to the Macintosh, updated for System 7. *(128 pages)*

THE LITTLE QUICKEYS BOOK
▲ *Stephen F. Roth and Don Sellers*
A handy guide to CE Software's QuicKeys 2.0 macro program. *(192 pges—available 10/91)*

THE LITTLE SYSTEM 7 BOOK
▲ *Kay Yarborough Nelson*
A clear, simple introduction to Apple's new operating system. Teach yourself the essentials of System 7, and skip the technical mumbo jumbo! *(160 pages)*

THE MACINTOSH FONT BOOK, 2nd Edition
▲ *Erfert Fenton*
Everything from font fundamentals to resolving ID conflicts, this book has long been acknowledged as the definitive guide to Mac fonts. Revised for TrueType and System 7. *(348 pp)*

THE MAC IS NOT A TYPEWRITER
▲ *Robin Williams*
Tips and techniques for producing beautiful typography with a computer. *(72 pages)*

PAGEMAKER 4: AN EASY DESK REFERENCE
▲ *Robin Williams*
A reference book that lets you look up how to do specific tasks with PageMaker 4. *(784 pp)*

THE QUARKXPRESS BOOK
▲ *David Blatner and Keith Stimely*
A comprehensive guide to QuarkXPress 3.0 and XTensions. *(534 pages)*

REAL WORLD FREEHAND 3
▲ *Olav Martin Kvern*
An insider's guide to the latest release of this popular Mac drawing program. *(512 pages)*

Order Form

phone: 800/283-9444 or 415/548-4393
fax: 415/548-5991

Quantity	Title	Price	Total
	Canned Art: Clip Art for the Macintosh (book only)	29.95	
	Canned Art: Clip Art for the Macintosh (book and disks)	39.95	
	Canvas 3.0: The Book	21.95	
	Database 101	18.95	
	HELP! The Art of Computer Technical Support	19.95	
	Learning PostScript: A Visual Approach	22.95	
	The Little Mac Book, 2nd Edition	12.95	
	The Little QuicKeys Book — *available 10/91*	14.95	
	The Little System 7 Book	12.95	
	The Macintosh Font Book, 2nd Edition	23.95	
	The Mac is not a typewriter	9.95	
	PageMaker 4: An Easy Desk Reference (Mac edition)	29.95	
	The QuarkXPress Book	24.95	
	Real World FreeHand 3	27.95	

Tax of 8% applies to California residents only.
UPS ground shipping: $4 for first item, $1 each additional.
UPS 2nd day air: $7 for first item, $2 each additional.
Air mail to Canada: $6 first item, $4 each additional.
Air mail overseas: $14 each item.

Subtotal	
8% Tax (CA only)	
Shipping	
TOTAL	

Name

Company

Address

City

State ____ Zip

Phone

☐ Check enclosed   ☐ Visa   ☐ MasterCard

☐ Company Purchase Order #

Credit Card Number

Expiration Date

Peachpit Press, Inc. ▲ 2414 Sixth St. ▲ Berkeley, CA 94710
Satisfaction unconditionally guaranteed or your money cheerfully refunded!